SO-BNE-331

ira Perspectives in Reading Series

INDOCTRINATE OR EDUCATE?

THOMAS C. HATCHER
and
LAWRENCE G. ERICKSON
Editors
West Virginia University

INTERNATIONAL READING ASSOCIATION
Newark, Delaware 19711

INTERNATIONAL READING ASSOCIATION

OFFICERS
1978-1979

President   Dorothy S. Strickland, Kean College of New Jersey, Union, New Jersey

Vice President   Roger Farr, Indiana University, Bloomington, Indiana

Vice President-Elect   Olive S. Niles, State Department of Education, Hartford, Connecticut

Executive Director   Ralph C. Staiger, International Reading Association, Newark, Delaware

DIRECTORS

Term Expiring Spring 1979

    Lou E. Burmeister, The University of Texas, El Paso, Texas
    Jack Cassidy, Millersville State College, Millersville, Pennsylvania
    Kenneth S. Goodman, University of Arizona, Tucson, Arizona

Term Expiring Spring 1980

    Mary Ann Baird, State Department of Education, Jackson, Mississippi
    Addie Stabler Mitchell, Morehouse College, Atlanta, Georgia
    Jean E. Robertson, University of Alberta, Edmonton, Alberta

Term Expiring Spring 1981

    Norma Dick, Clovis Unified School District, Clovis, California
    Eleanor M. Ladd, Temple University, Philadelphia, Pennsylvania
    John C. Manning, University of Minnesota, Minneapolis, Minnesota

Copyright 1979 by the
International Reading Association, Inc.

Library of Congress Cataloging in Publication Data

Main entry under title:
Indoctrinate or educate?
    (Perspectives in reading)
    Selected papers presented at the 21st Perspectives in
Reading Conference, Anaheim, 1976.
    Includes bibliographies.
    1. Reading—Congresses. I. Hatcher, Thomas C., 1939-
II. Erickson, Lawrence. III. International Reading
Association. IV. Perspectives in Reading Conference,
21st, Anaheim, Calif., 1976. V. Series.
LB1049.95.I52   428'.4   78-17802
ISBN 0-87207-120-0

ii

Contents

CONTRIBUTORS

Robert F. Baker
Ginn and Company
Lexington, Massachusetts

Lawrence G. Erickson
West Virginia University
Morgantown, West Virginia

Michele M. Fomalont
Green Bank School
Pocahontas County, West Virginia

Thomas C. Hatcher
West Virginia University
Morgantown, West Virginia

Adrienne Jones
Laguna Niguel, California

Elaine Lohr
Madison Public Schools
Madison, Wisconsin

Nell J. Segraves
Creation-Science Research Center
San Diego, California

Jo M. Stanchfield
Occidental College
Los Angeles, California

Foreword

How much freedom should teachers enjoy in the selection of reading matter and other sources of information and opinion for the classes they teach? Conversely, what rights do the voters of a school district have regarding the control of texts and other reading materials in their schools, especially if those printed sources seem to express concepts which are disturbing to certain groups of citizens in the community? Until the mid-seventies, the International Reading Association was not extensively involved in the controversies regarding censorship of instructional materials as a result of pressures applied by groups or individuals not on teaching staffs. Perhaps the Association, which has demonstrated such outstanding leadership in so many professional directions, has been so concerned with the processes and motivations for reading that it has not given much attention to certain aspects of the contents of the printed matter provided for young learners.

Unquestionably, many IRA members favor increased Association participation in social and political issues such as the censorship of schoolbooks by citizen pressure groups. Some of our "sister" associations have been maintaining crusades against the censorship of classroom reading matter by groups with special political or religious viewpoints. (In the United States, the American Library Association and the National Council of Teachers of English have spearheaded these crusades.) In any case, the publication of this book, *Indoctrinate or Educate?* represents a major step in the Association's interaction with the censorship problem.

Several of the contributors to this volume are employed in the educational agencies of the State of West Virginia, which is perhaps to be expected, since the most turbulent schoolbook censorship controversy of recent decades in North America occurred in

Kanawha County, West Virginia. Most of the other chapter authors also have had firsthand experience with classroom censorship as they have performed their respective professional roles, although understandably, they do not all view the problem in the same light. In fact, one of the strengths of this volume is the diversity of outlook of its authors, one third of whom are not professional educators.

On behalf of the Board of Directors and the Publications Committee of the International Reading Association, I want to thank all who have contributed to this book, and especially Thomas Hatcher and Lawrence Erickson, who first planned IRA's 1976 Perspectives Conference which focused on censorship in the schools, and who later edited the manuscript.

William Eller, President
International Reading Association
1977-1978

IRA PUBLICATIONS COMMITTEE 1978-1979 Harold L. Herber, Syracuse University, *Chairing* • Alison Bellack, Largo (Florida) C & I Center • Janet R. Binkley, IRA • Faye R. Branca, IRA • Norma Dick, Clovis (California) Unified School District • Roger Farr, Indiana University • Margaret Keyser Hill, Southern Illinois University • Jerry L. Johns, Northern Illinois University • Laura S. Johnson, Morton Grove, Illinois • Lloyd W. Kline, IRA • J. E. Merritt, The Open University • Christina Neal, St. Albans, West Virginia • Emma Rembert, Florida International University • James D. Riley, University of Montana • Lyndon W. Searfoss, Arizona State University • Cyrus F. Smith, Jr., University of Wisconsin at Milwaukee • Ralph C. Staiger, IRA • Mary Stainton, IRA • Judith N. Thelen, Frostburg State College • Carl J. Wallen, Arizona State University • Sam Weintraub, State University of New York at Buffalo.

The International Reading Association attempts, through its publications, to provide a forum for a wide spectrum of opinion on reading. This policy permits divergent viewpoints without assuming the endorsement of the Association.

Introduction

Every American school is faced with selecting and using reading materials which may conflict with the values of some community members. For many schools the conflict is barely discernible and short lived, but for some schools the conflict is widespread, intense, and sustained. The emergence of this issue in the 70s was addressed by the International Reading Association and the following resolution was adopted at the annual Delegates Assembly held at the 1975 IRA Convention in New York City.

WHEREAS
United States is a pluralistic society in which variability is the rule, not the exception, and throughout the two hundred year history of this democracy, the search for the common good has involved the examination of a wide variety of views; and

WHEREAS
evidence can be found on the ever-increasing variability of viewpoints regarding reading materials and teaching methods; and

WHEREAS
in light of recent developments regarding parent and educator involvement in textbook publication, selection, and usage, it is necessary to reaffirm a basic philosophic position which has been inherent in the use of textbooks since the founding of the United States, in that the democratic society is best served when the schools preserve the right of each individual to read a variety of materials which are of value and interest to him; and

WHEREAS
school systems, in selecting instructional materials, must promote a democratic spirit of cooperativeness and must seek to involve all those who will be affected by any materials selected for classroom use, then parents, teachers, administrators, students, textbook

authors, and publishers should be reminded of their democratic heritage and should resolve cooperatively to determine textbook selection procedures which will: 1) promote the underlying principles of a pluralistic society; 2) show concern for sound teaching and learning; 3) reassert the individual's right to read a wide variety of viewpoints; therefore be it

RESOLVED THAT
the International Reading Association convene a conference on textbook publication, selection, and usage which will encourage parents, students, educators, and publishers to propose textbook guidelines which represent a diversity of philosophic positions and which support a pluralistic society.

At the 1976 IRA Convention in Anaheim, California, the Twenty-First Perspectives in Reading Conference brought together authors, editors, publishers, teachers, parents, and reading authorities to share various viewpoints. This publication contains selected papers representing the viewpoints exchanged at the conference in Anaheim. The diverse papers which follow are intended to remind educators of the issues involved in the creation and use of reading materials in a pluralistic society.

TCH
LGE

Part One
Sociological and Educational
Perspectives on Reading Materials

The articles included in this publication address some of the issues involved in selecting and adopting reading textbooks for use in schools.

In Part 1, the Fomalont and Hatcher articles deal with aspects of the educational and sociological parameters of material selection. Fomalont begins her article with comments on the historical perspectives of material selection and then relates this to present sociological contexts, discussing controversies which have emerged in recent years. Hatcher asks the question, "What are the primary purposes of education?" and attempts to link textbook selection and adoption to his answer to this most important question. Hatcher's article is completed by his suggestion of recommendations which he feels should be followed by school systems in selecting instructional materials.

1

Reading Materials: The Sociological Context

Michele M. Fomalont

The articles included in this publication represent a wide range of views concerning the writing, publication, and selection of reading materials for use in school reading and language arts programs. One way of introducing these individual views of writer, publisher, educator, parent, or administrator is to examine the sociological backdrop against which decisions are made concerning reading materials.

To begin with, the materials themselves are social in nature. Regardless of whether they have been written expressly for classroom use or have been selected to fill some educational need, such materials reflect moral and ethical points of view, perhaps obvious or disguised prejudices, and/or cultural or ethnic backgrounds. Social bias can be reflected in a problem in a math book or a test item on an achievement test, as well as in works of literature or readings in the content areas.

We need only look through Nila Banton Smith's *American Reading Instruction (3)* to remind ourselves that reading materials have always reflected society's values and attitudes. The earliest primers used to teach children how to read were religious in content. Similarly, in later periods of American history, the patriotic and then moral-realistic tones of school texts reflected the changes in the purposes for schooling as the nation grew and expanded its world role. We can trace the various periods down to the present, observing that each period produced materials that were reflections of the prevailing social atmosphere and were, in turn, meant to perpetuate those values that society held dear. Nothing demonstrates this sociological context more visibly than the changes in basal readers that have taken place over the decades. Our increased social awareness, resulting from the minority movements of this period, led to considerable research into the middle-class bias of school reading materials. These investigations, in turn, resulted in extensive modifications so that today's texts show a cultural diversity unknown in earlier materials. In her article in this publication, Jo M. Stanchfield discusses the current research in reading interests of boys and girls. The results of this research will bring changes in reading materials of the future.

We take these reading materials, which are undeniably products of our social climate, and put them before social beings— the readers. Their ethnic group memberships, social classes, economic levels, educational opportunities, and achievements will all determine how they will react to the materials before them. And because it is widely accepted that children will interact in some way with what they read, concern has always been expressed over the role reading materials play in shaping mental and social growth.

Today's school children read not only carefully constructed textbooks that meet prescribed educational objectives but also read an enormous amount of so-called supplementary materials, all of which (it is assumed) will provide them with healthy and realistic views of themselves, broaden their outlooks, and extend their abilities to think objectively. It was precisely this belief in the importance of materials in forming healthy self-concepts that publishers responded to by producing materials that show not only the nation's cultural diversity but tell the "real" story of life today. This means that considerably more language arts textbooks, literature anthologies, or supplementary readings contain stories told in dialect as well as unexpurgated language or express a point of view at odds with the moral beliefs of many Americans. The motivation for using such materials is that the schools no longer play the hypocrite by presenting a view different from what children already know or will find out once they enter the social mainstream as adults. Instead of shielding children from the facts of American society, the idea is to present the facts and to try to develop some reasoning process so that children will be able to come to moral grips with the problems involved.

As a result of acceptance of this philosophy, reading materials changed drastically during the late sixties and early seventies. Because of the nature of the new readings, many parents educated in the public school system were shocked. In the past, it had been unquestioned that schools would maintain "proper" moral and social perspectives; today, this assumption is no longer widespread. Some feel that the attempt to cater to minority demands and to tell it "as it really is" has gone too far. These parents are not certain that exposing their children to controversial materials, such as those dealing with street problems, etc., is the way to end the hypocrisy of text materials. Furthermore, some contend that the parent, and not the school, has the responsibility for dealing with controversial subjects. A basic misunderstanding, which resulted from many textbook adoptions, was that materials are used at the discretion of the teacher and are not required readings in all cases. Controversial materials become part of the adoption process because, as readings, they will be available to students if and when the teacher wishes to use them.

A controversy in Kanawha County, West Virginia, began with objections to the trend toward realism in school reading materials. One of the statements made by the anti-textbook people was that such readings offer "distorted" and "surrealistic" views because they are not always presented in a program which provides a balance of views. Even if such readings were totally true, the question is whether it is necessary to show America's blemishes or whether we should " ... give our children hope and promise that with God's grace and wisdom they may one day see our nation and world as it should be"(1). This is not just the cry of a militant minority, such as those who protested the texts in Kanawha County, but the honest belief of a growing number of concerned educators and parents.

As a result of the controversies involving textbooks, two camps of thought have polarized: those who believe that a program of varied readings, honestly exposing children to all facets of the culture, will enhance their capacities to determine their own liberal and humanistic values and attitudes; and those who believe that such a wide-open approach may impugn values or attitudes which run contrary to America's vision of morality. Reading materials are just one of many aspects of the school curriculum that have come into the spotlight. The schools have a grave responsibility for improving the nation's moral condition. When it comes to reading materials, the problem becomes one of who will make the selections and, if there is a conflict over the choices to be made, how it will be resolved. It is notable that more and more parents are refusing to be disenfranchised in the determination of curriculum and materials, despite the existence of elected school boards. This development seems to say that schools have become remote from the society they serve and that a new look must be given to the moral role they play.

The selection of reading materials for school children can be viewed in many different ways. In her review of textbook selection procedures in the Madison, Wisconsin, public schools, Elaine Lohr makes the important point that materials can be selected only after educational objectives are carefully defined, and that there must be a procedure available for those who would take issue with any particular reading. If we cannot resolve the different points of view over educational goals, then perhaps the nation's public schools may have to offer a variety of objectives to satisfy all of its constituents. In any case, the criteria used for writing materials for children, for their selection for publication, and for their adoption will all need to be reevaluated. Many of the articles in this publication concern themselves precisely with this process.

One might first consider the moral and ethical guidelines an author uses in writing children's literature. Adrienne Jones discusses the honesty and integrity which must motivate such an author. Jo M. Stanchfield speaks of the criteria set forth by Hazard. These include a sense of beauty in children's stories, a share in great human emotions, a balance of seriousness with play, a commitment to books of knowledge, and a concern for "profound morality." Robert Baker sets forth the publisher's guidelines for textbooks and other reading materials. These guidelines, according to Baker, have always reflected the demands of educators and will no doubt be influenced by social trends if such trends command attention. For example, Nell Segraves proposes legislative ways by which the so-called "secular" orientation of present-day curriculum and materials will be balanced with an awareness of the role of religion in civilization. Such legislation will need to be observed by publishers.

As for the adoption process itself, Lawrence G. Erickson and Michele M. Fomalont discuss the criteria for the evaluation of reading materials by textbook adoption committees. Such criteria should take into consideration internal factors already present in the materials, as well as external factors such as school philosophy and goals. In its study of the Kanawha County controversy, the NEA concluded that much more needs to be done by the school system to communicate its views to the public, and that parents should be able to play an advisory role in its curriculum decisions (2). Too often, in the past, complaints about materials were not seriously reviewed until after the selection had been made. How well a school allows for the adequate input of teachers, parents, other professionals, and laypersons in materials selection will determine the success with which these materials are accepted and used. Otherwise, taxpayers may continue to vote down school bonds or, worse, commit the kinds of civil disruptions that took place in West Virginia.

Thomas C. Hatcher presents four broad guidelines for dealing with the cultural diversity that confronts school curriculum decision making. In addition to broad guidelines, Lawrence Erickson discusses school-community relations and presents a number of ways for schools to build trust and public support.

The many points of view in the articles presented in this publication ultimately demonstrate that materials will always play a dual role in education. On the one hand, they are curriculum tools necessary for implementing educational objectives, and their use will determine their worth. On the other hand, the materials, themselves, shape and determine the values of the curriculum. Fully understanding these roles will help clarify many decisions concerning the use of reading materials for our schools.

References
1. Mathews, John. "Access Rights to Children's Minds: Texts of Our Times," *New Republic*, January 4 and 11, 1975, 21.
2. National Education Association. *Inquiry Report: Kanawha County, West Virginia—A Textbook Study in Cultural Conflict.* Washington, D.C.: The Association, February 1975, 59-62.
3. Smith, Nila Banton. *American Reading Instruction.* Newark, Delaware: International Reading Association, 1965.

Indoctrinate or Educate:
An Educational Perspective on the Use of Materials

Thomas C. Hatcher

The recent controversy regarding textbook selection, adoption, and usage has prompted many reactions from individuals and groups regarding the impact of book selection on students. The thrusts of these reactions have generally been negative and have implied the belief that teachers, through the use of the materials in class, are corrupting the moral standards of students and are prompting students to disagree with and to disavow the precepts taught to them by parents.

In this outcry, teachers have been characterized as liberalized conveyers of moral concepts which depart from traditional viewpoints. As users of textbooks selected by school districts, teachers have been viewed as totally supporting many of the ideas included within textbooks with which some parents disagree.

The sad commentary is that parents have apparently been able to browbeat teachers, since there have been few attempts by teachers to explain how materials are being used and to educate parents as to why materials which present differing viewpoints are necessary as a part of a school reading-language arts curriculum.

The following comments will be an attempt to explain what I consider to be an educational perspective on the use of controversial materials and, in the process, to give at least one illustration of how most teachers probably approach classroom use of reading-language arts materials.

The reader must understand that this article is written from the standpoint of an educator and in defense of the educational processes. As a teacher and a parent, I do question some of the content inclusions of some textbooks and agree that publishers and authors should not have included these selections in their publications. I do feel, however, that the vast majority of selections, with which some parent groups have found fault, are not questionable in terms of content and/or in terms of how teachers use them in the classroom.

PRIMARY PURPOSE OF EDUCATION

It would appear that an educational perspective on the use of so-called "controversial" materials cannot be adequately dealt with until an understanding of the primary purpose of education is gained.

If one reads one of the latest statements from the Education Policies Commission on the purposes of American education *(1)*, it is clear that most educators would agree that the primary purpose of education is to produce "a rational thinking individual, who has developed both critical and creative thinking, and who uses these intellectual abilities in becoming a useful and productive member of society."

EDUCATIONAL PERSPECTIVES

If schools accept this purpose as their primary reason for existence, it is clear that higher level thinking processes must be emphasized in school curricular activities. In recent years, there has been a change in that direction. While the basic school curricular content is much the same today as it was ten to twenty years ago, the type and frequency of higher level thinking skills incorporated into instruction in school subject matter areas have changed. At one time, teachers predominantly emphasized the teaching of lower level thinking abilities. Since the early 1960s, however, a trend has started to not only continue the teaching of these basic skills but to provide for the pupil's development of higher level thinking processes. Developmental activities to enhance the interpretative, critical, and creative processes have been incorporated into the textbooks of not only reading but science, social studies, language arts, math, and other curricular areas. The intent is to recognize and support the premise that rational thinking processes must be emphasized and that, in so doing, individuals ultimately will be the primary beneficiaries as they will be better able (than students of previous years) to control their destinies and to react intelligently to the many complicated facets of American life.

To provide for the development of higher level thinking skills and abilities means that the teacher must utilize both processes and

8

materials which promote problem solving, inquiry, discovery, brainstorming, debates, and open-ended discussions. Higher level critical and creative thinking cannot be developed with materials which do not lend themselves to having students react, question, propose, analyze, and evaluate. Nor can critical and creative thinking be developed and enhanced without delving into the problems of our society. If the latter occurs, the students will be encouraged to seek perspectives on issues, standards, morals, ethics, and problems which, from an educational point of view, means that all sides of any question at hand will be presented, discussed, and evaluated and the students will be helped to form their own opinions and viewpoints regarding issues and problems where there is no "right" answer. The teacher, as a curricular developer, serves as a facilitator of action and as a promoter of critical and creative thinking and not as a promoter or indoctrinator of certain points of view.

It is precisely this last point that has been grossly misunderstood in the 1975-1976 textbook revolt. Too frequently, parents saw teachers as indoctrinators of concepts, rather than as facilitators of higher level thinking. Teachers were accused of promoting certain viewpoints which were divergent from the views held by some parental groups.

The outcry was so pressurized that many teachers failed in helping parents to understand that indoctrination was not the case in point and that what was really occurring was that students were being taught to think critically and creatively through the use of materials which, for the most part, did not question or degrade certain moral and ethical precepts held by particular groups of parents. The stories in the materials to which parents objected during the textbook revolt were largely stories about American problems and issues for which there are no "right" or "wrong" answers. In addition, these stories were included in readers intended for junior and senior high school students who are at an age where open-ended reading selections can be utilized to help them become more cognizant of our melting pot society, where opinions are quite diverse, and where, as Americans, we are taught to respect the viewpoints of others. If parents know and understand what teachers do as they work with students, they will realize that teachers do not indoctrinate but, rather, serve as developers and facilitators of the type of high level thinking indicative of an individual who keeps all options open and who is receptive to the varying viewpoints of others. If our schools cannot serve this purpose, then just what is their function?

I would like to discuss from the teacher's perspective how he or she might deal with one story which was considered controversial by a group of parents in West Virginia. The reader must realize that I have selected only one story, from many, considered inappropriate. The story is one for which major reservations were expressed but which I, as an educator, feel is quite satisfactory for the purpose of helping to develop a rational thinker.

The story, "What to Do About Draft Card Burners" by Henry G. Felsen (2), was included in a tenth grade literature-reading anthology. The selection was written by the author to his son in the Marine Corps.

Basically, the thoughts expressed in the selection relate the father's reaction to what should be done to people who defy their government and burn their draft cards. While the author admits that those who burn their draft cards should suffer the penalty specified by law, he indicates that the problem is one much deeper than just putting these individuals in jail. In discussing why some men have chosen to publicly burn their draft cards, he relates that such individuals have probably done so in good conscience. The author asks, "What do we do with these draft card burners?" "...if we punish people for daring to disagree with the policies of the government, where do we stop?" he questions. "The excuse now is a war. But once you deny free citizenship for one cause, it's always easy to find another. And to punish people for holding unpopular political ideas leads to punishing them for belonging to 'unpopular' religious, racial, or other minorities."

In attempting to bring perspective to the dilemma of what to do with draft card burners, who can be looked upon as being both right and wrong in their actions, Felsen (2) ends the letter to his son with the following:

> Your conscience led you to the field, with a rifle. Another boy's conscience leads him to burn his draft card in a protest against warring. Each of you, in your own way, is performing the noblest duty of a free citizen. Each of you is right. But which of you is the more right, only time will tell.

In analyzing the contents of this selection and the manual directions to the teacher, it is apparent that the story was included to solicit critical and creative thinking from the reader. The manual encourages teachers to ask students to give their reactions to the article, to debate the issue which the author poses, and to consider government policies which relate to freedoms we enjoy as

Americans. The manual suggests that teachers might want their students to review the May 1968 U.S. Supreme Court decision on draft card burning, as well as to read parts of Supreme Court Justice Abe Fortas' book, *Concerning Dissent and Civil Disobedience.*

REACTIONS TO CASE ILLUSTRATION

It is clear to this educator that the article and the accompanying directions to the teacher are consistent with what is considered to be the major purpose of American education at this time. In using this selection in class, teachers who have been well trained in how to deal with open-ended reading selections will know that the primary intent is to promote rational thinking but, since the story is open-ended, the ultimate goal is for students to make their own judgments regarding where they stand on this particular issue. To me, this is what education is all about. It is not indoctrination but, rather, is far from it. In America, our citizenry is free to make its own decisions and our schools exist to help us meet this end. If school systems are forced to stop using open-ended reading selections and, at the same time, to abstain from the promotion of critical and creative thinking among students, then we might ask how long our freedoms will continue to exist. Schools have been a major force in preserving our basic rights as Americans and, as such, must continue to utilize open-ended reading selections.

RECOMMENDATIONS

I feel that teachers understand why certain types of reading selections are incorporated into readers. Similarly, I feel that the majority of parents also have this basic understanding. In reviewing the 1975-1976 textbook protests, it is apparent that not *all* parents clearly perceive what education is attempting to accomplish and that the development of higher level thinking skills and abilities is very much a part of the educational process. As educators, we are not attempting to develop individuals who will disavow the beliefs held by their parents but, rather, we are helping to develop individuals who will be open minded, critical, creative, and questioning and who will respect the views of others on issues which have no right or wrong answers.

Parents need to fully perceive the intent of this direction, and it is the responsibility of school systems to develop the strategies necessary to see that educational goals and objectives are clear and are understood. Parents, students, and teachers must all be actively involved in setting these directions and in selecting materials which will meet basic purposes of American education. School systems and teachers also have the responsibility of developing necessary educational programs which will encourage parents to be advocates instead of adversaries.

Most of the materials to which parents protested in 1975-1976 were very much related to and consistent with the purposes of American education. Who would question our attempts, as educators, to produce rational thinkers? Perhaps it is only those who misunderstand the purposes of American education. As teachers, we can alter this with the right strategies. The following suggestions might help with this problem:

1. School systems must assume an active role in helping to structure parent education programs which will promote an understanding of the system's educational goals.
2. A wide variety of media—letters, open forum discussions, newspapers, radio, and television—must be utilized in communicating with parents. Too many school systems make the mistake of using only one outlet for communication, even though it is known that people react very differently to various forms of communication.
3. Teachers must communicate with their students, in an active way and through a variety of media, about the major goals of a particular class or set of experiences.
4. School systems must insure active participation of parents and students on important school committees: specifically, curriculum, textbook adoption and selection, and program evaluation. Parental reactions and reports should be given periodically to all other parents not involved on committees.
5. Each school should make use of parent expertise in developing particular aspects of any school experience. Parents can be definite assets and they will volunteer quite readily if we, as educators, reach them.
6. Textbook materials being considered for adoption should be placed in strategic locations in public libraries and in local schools (on a rotational basis) for parents to evaluate and react to.
7. Open hearings on textbook adoption and selection should be held before final selections are made so that parents feel they have opportunities to have input.
8. Teachers must be prepared to defend openly the final recommendations made in adopting textbooks and should take a leadership role in doing so.

The above are but a few of the steps which teachers and school systems can take to promote good public relations regarding procedures of textbook adoption and selection and the methods being used in handling textbook selections in the classroom.

References

1. Educational Policies Commission. *The Central Purpose of American Education*. Washington, D.C.: National Education Association, 1962, 12.
2. Felsen, Henry G. "What to Do about Draft Card Burners" in Robert C. Pooley, et al. (Eds.), *Perspectives*. Chicago: Scott, Foresman, 1963, 1969, 119-123.

Part Two

Author and Publisher Perspectives

In Part 2 of this volume, an attempt is made to present author and publisher perspectives on issues involving material selection. Jones, who is a children's literature author, looks at the problem from the standpoint of an author, suggesting that censorship is a danger and should be questioned. Stanchfield, a professor in the areas of education and children's literature, speaks out on the role of literature and its place in the education of youth. Stanchfield's article suggests standards which can be utilized in selecting literature for use in books for children. Baker, who is president of Ginn and Company, relates the textbook selection controversies to parameters which impinge on publishers and provides insight into decision making at his level of operation.

The three articles in Part 2 do not provide full answers to all questions which could be asked regarding author and publisher responsibilities in the publication of instructional textbooks. The writers' ideas, however, do stimulate one to think about author and publisher roles and the linkages which must occur between and among authors, publishers, school systems, and parents of children who use textbooks.

Values, Themes, and Censorship: The Writer's View

Adrienne Jones

A great deal of correspondence is involved in arranging a conference such as the one held in Anaheim, California, by the International Reading Association in May 1976. In one of the letters replying to a question of mine, I was asked what values and themes are presented in my stories. Now, when a writer whose real delight lies in "telling a story" is asked about the values and themes in her writing, a terrible fog descends on her brain and a long, long silence ensues. Surely, one assures oneself, values and themes *are* present. In trying to find some solution to this dilemma, I mulled over such words as brotherhood and love and courage and many other good and noble nouns. But they were only words and conveyed little of my intent.

Still, the question of values and themes was there and surely an answer could be found. I continued searching my mind, bravely pressing on, for courage must be the watchword of any writer of fiction. Freelance fiction writing is about as risky an occupation as one may find, and without courage one is nowhere. I decided to plunge right in, hoping during the discourse to discover, in a slightly roundabout way, the answer to the values and themes problem.

As you know, there are as many ways of approaching a piece of writing as there are writers. Undoubtedly, some of us have a very firm hold on any underlying message. But for others, the only conscious thought is of the story itself. Sometimes it begins with characters, sometimes with place, sometimes with plot—whatever grabs one's fancy. Next, there is an effort to produce the story with integrity and honesty on paper. One should view with some suspicion the writer whose first question is, "Yes, but will it sell?" or whose first remark is, "*They* want Westerns or Gothics or Stories of the Twenties this year, so you're crazy to write about a girl whose grandmother lives alone and is sinking into senility."

So back to the word, integrity. If the grandmother story is the one that boils and bubbles in the mind and creates that necessary feeling of vital excitement in the writer, then it seems to me that is the story that should be written. This is where courage comes in. The writer must risk himself to do this, for it is quite possible he will *not* sell the girl/grandmother story. But it is a risk writers should take, or we diminish the whole offering that should be made to readers. Otherwise, we will have an occasional original piece and a thousand copyists. Young readers deserve better than a stunted choice. There should be the widest offering possible, and this is obtained by each writer working in good faith to present himself, his knowledge, his unique place in life to his readers. Several poets, in the past, have worded this simply and well: Emerson, *The only gift is a portion of thyself*; Whitman, *When I give, I give myself*; James Russell Lowell, *The gift without the giver is bare.*

As to values and themes, if a story is honestly written, the values in life that are important to the author will show through, but they must be discerned by the reader and translated into his own terms. Thus the meaning behind the story will vary considerably from reader to reader, depending on what each brings to the story. The writer brings some things to it but the reader supplies the rest.

Another question that should be touched upon is the one of censorship, for the censor stands between writer and reader and can bring to naught even a good and honest effort. It is true there are certain things a writer should watch: he should not misrepresent his own expertise in a given field; claim to be that which he is not; nor lack diligence in research of anything presented as fact, whether enclosed in a work of fiction or presented openly as fact in nonfiction. If these basics are properly regarded, when we come to the question of censorship, the problem is already solved insofar as the writer is concerned. If he is presenting material—fiction or nonfiction—with an effort to reveal as much of the subject or character or story or locale as is possible within the bounds of good writing and style, then censorship should not enter his mind. Whether writing for children or adults, *the writer's integrity is to his material.*

To put the subject of censorship as precisely and concisely as possible:

1. During the creative process, the writer should not censor himself nor be censored from outside. This is the most certain way to narrow or kill true creativity.

2. At the publishing level, a certain amount of picking and choosing and rejecting is necessary. But this should not be confused with censorship. The publishing trade should turn out as wide a range of books as possible. If the overall picture is taken into account, they do marvelously well. As to the individual editor's work—in discussion with the writer, he should iron out any difficulties concerning good taste while retaining the integrity of the work. An editor should reject a work that is unsuitable; for example, a picture book for the preschool group that deals with homosexuality—not because mention of homosexuality is taboo, but because the preschooler has no concept of this subject and no need or ability to deal with it.

3. Within the family, the parents should censor for their own children. Only a parent knows what is acceptable within the confines of that particular family. Outside censorship can deprive children who are ready for certain concepts or knowledge that might be unacceptable to some other family. Or even unacceptable to the censor!

4. School texts should be chosen by people who are knowledgeable in the field and have broad experience in education and an understanding of this present day world. Textbooks must serve the needs of the students and prepare them as well as possible to deal with this exciting but complex life. It is fine for school boards to listen to community voices, but unwise for them to be ruled by any clique advocating narrow or warped views and wishing to censor textbook choice to support those views. For example, there have been groups of people who have objected to texts simply because they revealed facts about history that did not adhere to a popular or local mythology.

5. As to overall censorship, the first amendment to the Constitution is quite clear in the matter. *Congress shall make no law ... abridging the freedom of speech, or of the press.* From time to time, it is brought to our attention that censorship of the press is the first tool of any repressive government.

In years past, life was much simpler for writers. There used to be a very acceptable way of dealing with the dangers of censorship. You must remember that, for the written word, that handy little star—the asterisk—served the same purpose as does "expletive deleted" for the tape recorded word. Recently, I ran across the following eight lines that make it clear how easy it all was for the writer early in this century. The author of this little verse was the gentlemen who wrote, "There's a long long trail a-winding into the land of my dreams." His name was Stoddard King and he died in 1933.

> A writer owned an Asterisk,
> And kept it in his den,
> Where he wrote tales (which had large sales)
> Of frail and erring men;
> And always, when he reached the point
> Where carping censors lurk,
> He called upon the Asterisk
> To do his dirty work.

Trends—Not Destiny

Jo M. Stanchfield

The terms *pluralistic, multiethnic, intercultural,* and *nonsexist* have become household words in a society which has grown to recognize and respond to the needs and rights of its minorities. During the past fifteen years, various liberation movements have focused attention on discrimination and inequality in all areas of American life. The field of education has been a center of controversy. A prominent issue has been that of discrimination and bias in children's reading materials.

In the early years of the civil rights movement, educators began to reevaluate instructional materials in light of the changing social scene. Traditional materials, oriented to traditional white middle-class standards of the majority population, were condemned for racist and sexist stereotypes. Also criticized was the lack of material offering positive images for minority children. The social implications of this imbalance were apparent to concerned educators, who recognized the effect it could have upon children's self-concepts.

Attempts to achieve ethnic and sex balance have created a demand for curricular materials which accurately portray minorities and realistically present the multicultural character of our society. Authors and publishers of textbooks and trade books have accepted the responsibility for revising objectionable content and for developing new materials to meet the new standards. Sincere efforts have been made to provide readers with materials that show minorities in varied, realistic, and favorable life situations. Recognition has also been given to the rich cultural heritages of America's varied ethnic groups, and materials dealing with these subjects have been included in textbooks and added to library collections.

All of these measures have helped to provide a balanced view of all segments of our society—a view that offers all children the opportunity to identify in a positive and realistic way with models of their own age, sex, race, or social class. As this encouraging trend continues, it is important that educators wisely control the swing of the pendulum. Those responsible for providing, selecting, and censoring children's reading materials should remember the proverbial admonition, "Don't throw out the baby with the bath water." They must eliminate gross abuses of bias, prejudice, stereotypes, and negative images. However, they must not become so overawed by the advocates of balance that they purge our classrooms and libraries of worthwhile books, simply because the content does not conform to standards of the contemporary social climate.

James Harvey *(3)*, writing for *The School Library Journal*, quotes a legal decision which covers this aspect of censorship. In dismissing a taxpayer's suit, which attempted to suppress the reading of *Oliver Twist* and *The Merchant of Venice* on the grounds of anti-Semitism, the judge ruled:

> Public interest in a free and democratic society does not warrant or encourage the suppression of any books at the whim of an unduly sensitive person or persons, merely because a character described in such a book as belonging to a particular race or religion is portrayed in a derogatory or offensive manner.

Authors and publishers have a responsibility to provide children with books that offer positive images of minorities. They also have a responsibility to the total group of children who read and learn. Children should not be deprived of the ability to think for themselves and to make value judgments. Controversial literature can be a valuable tool for teaching social and moral values, and should not be arbitrarily eliminated from our classrooms.

While racial and ethnic minorities formed the vanguard of the social revolution, women's liberation groups have actively joined the equal rights movement. From an educational viewpoint, however, the issue of sexism involves more than the eradication of traditional sex roles in which both girls and boys are stereotyped. It is true that traditional images can create a devastating handicap for girls and boys whose natures and abilities take them out of the norm, according to socially assigned roles. There is a need for more realistic characterization in children's literature. At the same time, educators, authors, and publishers should not overlook the fact that, if boys and girls are to be equal in the learning process, sex differences must be taken into consideration. This is vitally important in learning to read. Experimental research, as well as teacher observation, has shown that boys are not as effective readers as girls. Research has also shown that boys *will* learn to read if their learning problems are understood and if instruction and materials meet their interests and abilities.

One of the major sex differences is that of reading interests. The writer's studies of children's interests and achievement in sex-segregated groups showed that girls' reading interests cover a wide range of subjects, including many that are generally considered to be boy-oriented. Boys, on the other hand, have interests that call for reading materials with the appeal of the unusual and the dynamic. They are motivated to read by stories of action and excitement. Out of fifty subject categories, those most preferred by boys include adventure and exploration, sports and games, outdoor life, science fiction, space exploration, sea adventure, fantasy, humor, and mystery. Most-favored story characteristics for boys are unusual experiences, excitement, suspense, liveliness and action, surprise or unexpectedness, fanciful or weird elements, and funny incidents *(5)*.

With these literary elements in mind, authors and publishers can provide reading materials which appeal to both boys and girls. These high interest subjects offer opportunities to show girls and women in varied and unusual roles. While boys show little interest in stories with female characters in the traditional backgrounds of home or school, they do enjoy reading about girls in exciting roles. Two highly preferred books are Scott O'Dell's *Island of the Blue Dolphins* and Jean George's *Julie of the Wolves*. In these favorites, the lone heroines display qualities of courage, ingenuity, and resourcefulness in unusual and exciting situations.

Authors and publishers have a responsibility to see that children's reading materials have not only appropriate social values but also worthwhile literary qualities. Egoff (2) comments on mediocrity in children's literature in her article, "If That Don't Do No Good, That Won't Do No Harm":

> The role of literature is to help develop the individual, and it takes a good book to do this. A poor book takes a child and puts him back a step or two, a mediocre book takes a child and leaves him where he is. A good book promotes an awareness of the possibilities of life, the universality of life, the awakening of response.

Burns, Broman, and Lowe *(1)* reinforce the view that good literature is essential in providing real and vicarious experiences for children in a constantly changing world. They state, "The one guiding principle that applies to all children is to use good literature—books that have enduring quality, that appeal to many levels, that can be appreciated by the adult as well as the child."

To preserve the quality of children's reading materials during the current era of reevaluation and censorship, the literary criteria of Paul Hazard can be constructive. His five standards will help authors and publishers maintain the quality of excellence in the face of pressures that could lead to increasing mediocrity of content.

Hazard (4) commends books that "offer children an intuitive and direct way of knowledge, simple beauty capable of being perceived immediately, arousing in their souls a vibration which will endure all their lives." This criterion again calls to mind the beautiful story, *Julie of the Wolves*, with its powerful word imagery of the tundra. Taro Yashima's *Crow Boy* provides another rich experience for young readers.

A second Hazard criterion stresses the values of books that enable children to share great human emotions and "teach them not to despise everything that is mysterious in creation and in man." Outstanding examples of this category are *The Velveteen Rabbit* by Margery Bianco, *Call It Courage* by Armstrong Sperry, and *Johnny Tremain* by Esther Forbes.

Hazard's third criterion shows his awareness of the need for balance in life. He cites, "Books which respect the valor and eminent dignity of play; which understand that the training of intelligence and reason cannot and must not always have the immediately useful and practical as its goal." The factors of play, humor, and fun-for-fun's-sake are important in maintaining a healthy emotional climate for children. Books that offer this change of pace include Edward Lear's *Complete Nonsense Book*, Bennet Cerf's *Book of Riddles*, and Elaine Konigsberg's *From the Mixed-Up Files of Mrs. Basil E. Frankweiler*.

In his fourth standard, Hazard pays homage to books of knowledge—books that do not pretend to teach without drudgery. He states that students must be resigned to the fact that there are things which cannot be learned without great effort. He softens the aspect of "drudgery" by suggesting that books of knowledge should have "tact and moderation ... instead of pouring out so much material on a child's soul, they [should rather] plant in it a seed that will develop from the inside ...." Finally, he expresses his liking for books that "do not claim that knowledge can take the place of everything else ... [that] distill from all different kinds of knowledge the most difficult and the most necessary—that of the human heart." Informational books that meet this standard are *Pyramid* by David Macaulay and *Growing Up Green* by Skelsey and Huckaby.

Hazard's fifth standard for the selection of children's books relates to morality:

> I like books that contain a profound morality...books that set in action truths worthy of lasting forever, and of inspiring one's whole inner life; those demonstrating that an unselfish and faithful love always ends by finding its reward, be it only in oneself; how ugly and low are envy, jealousy and greed; how people who utter only slander and lies end by coughing up vipers and toads whenever they speak. In short, I like books that have the integrity to perpetuate their own faith in truth and justice.

In this final category are such classics as *Charlotte's Web* by E. B. White, *The Little Prince* by Antoine De Saint Exupery, and *Black Beauty* by Anna Sewell.

Authors and publishers can rely on Hazard's criteria as sound guidelines for developing new reading material for children. If the values expressed in his standards were followed faithfully, there would be a greater awareness of the impact of literature on children's lives and, perhaps, less need for future censorship in terms of moral or social values.

References
1. Burns, Paul C., Betty L. Broman, and Alberta L. Lowe. *The Language Arts in Childhood Education*. Chicago: Rand McNally, 1971.
2. Egoff, Sheila. "If That Don't Do No Good, That Won't Do No Harm: The Uses and Dangers of Mediocrity in Children's Reading," *School Library Journal*, October 1972.
3. Harvey, James. "Acting for the Children?" *School Library Journal*, February 1973.
4. Hazard, Paul. *Books, Children, and Men*. Boston: Horn Book, 1960.
5. Stanchfield, Jo M. *Sex Differences in Learning to Read*. Bloomington, Indiana: Phi Delta Kappa Educational Foundation, 1973.

A Publisher Views the Development and Selection of Reading Programs

Robert F. Baker

Perhaps some communities in this country have seen "burnings" of basal readers as they have, regrettably, seen burnings of books written for adults. Perhaps somewhere, too, elementary school personnel have lost community respect (if not tenured positions) because they insisted on teaching a particular reading program. Certainly, there have been occasional court cases dealing with the rights of school personnel to select particular titles or the rights of parents to object to the selections. But such overt censorship cases are relatively infrequent with respect to reading materials used in elementary school programs. The basic civil liberties guaranteed by the First Amendment—the right to read, the right to publish—seem only indirectly related to choices of school books that by law are to be determined by local school authorities and their designated professional representatives. Rather, the determination of what is included and what is not included in school reading materials is influenced by less direct pressure and more judgmental influence.

A review of these concerns must begin with noting certain differences in the use and selection of different kinds of reading materials; some of the present national and local concerns that influence the nature of these materials today; and, finally, some of the approaches that publishers use to cope with these complex concerns.

It is important at the outset to distinguish among three kinds of reading materials because each is subject to different selection procedures and, hence, to somewhat different community pressures. First, of course, are basic instructional materials intended for use by all children in a classroom. These are the major conveyors of instruction. Because such programs are intended for use by all children and any child engaged in progressing through the instructional sequence does not easily have the option of avoiding "Reader 3" or "Reader 8," the content and instruction carried by such titles are examined carefully by school officials and, increasingly, by parent and community groups concerned with maintaining appropriate standards. Inasmuch as most basal programs are created for potential use with about 80 percent of the children (all but the very accelerated and the very limited), such programs must possess broad general appeal. They must clearly present content that interests and excites a substantial plurality of American parents, teachers, and children, while at the same time serve the essential instructional purpose. But to do this they must also reduce to a minimum any content elements objectionable to substantial groups of Americans. It is with respect to such basal programs that many of my subsequent observations are addressed.

At least two other kinds of reading materials are selected by the schools. Many publishers develop a large variety of supplementary programs to satisfy particular learning needs. Ranging from small packages of individual titles designed for enrichment or guided practice in reading to multimedia kits designed to reinforce or extend basic skills, such supplementary programs are intended primarily for use by individuals or special groups of children. For this reason, such publications frequently are subject to less detailed study by selection committees than are the major basal programs. They tend to be planned with the needs of particular youngsters in mind; for instance, a series of supplemental bilingual-bicultural readers designed for practice by youngsters developing competence in reading English.

Trade books constitute the third important segment of reading materials for children. Like all literature written to delight and inform, such titles are created with little direct instructional purpose. Most are selected for school and classroom library use by informed librarians and specialists guided by major book reviews and by general community guidelines—quality, taste, and children's interests. The very volume of such publications militates against detailed analysis of content; but more important is the way in which such titles are used as independent reading. Seldom is any child required to read a particular title; if a parent questions the value of a particular book, the teacher can easily substitute another. Thus, although total library collections and classroom collections may be expected to reflect the values of a particular community, individual titles are freed from the requirement of serving the complex array of values one finds in an American social setting.

What are these values? What are the concerns that affect the selection of text and graphics material? Most Americans seem to feel that the basic reading programs intended for use by children should reflect the pluralistic, multicultural, multivalued, mosaic of American life today. The programs must be nonracist and nonsexist, offering children insights into varied patterns of family life, experiences with literature of many kinds, and introductions to our rich and diverse heritage from many cultures of the world. Such programs should gradually help children read selections of increasing depth and maturity, introduce them to major American writers for children, sufficiently stimulate their imaginations so they will want to continue reading, and avoid elements of any language inappropriate to children's levels of maturity.

Few publishers, teachers, or parents would have difficulty agreeing on such guiding principles; it is in the execution that publishers experience difficulty.

What is the appropriate cultural mix that should appear in any single reader? Between black and white Americans? Mexican-Americans and Puerto Ricans? Asian, Italian, Jewish, or Native Americans, and other ethnic groups? Does a one thousand-year-old Korean folktale have to be balanced within the covers of a single title with a portrait of an Asian-American family today to avoid stereotyping an ancient and honorable culture? What is the range of skin colors that must appear in our graphics reproduction to avoid giving the children the impression that all blacks look alike? How does one convey in readers the range of occupational choices open to women in the world today? How does one cope with the backlash from mothers who find aprons and ironing boards disappearing from children's books and are unhappy with the portrait of family life that results?

- Is *Three Billy Goats Gruff* a sexist title?
- Where can publishers find more literature by and about Chicanos which is appropriate for the fourth grade child?
- Does *Little House on the Prairie* reflect traditional middle-class values and, if so, should not such values be represented in our readers along with values of other kinds?

Such issues are representative of those faced by publishers, authors, and graphics designers as they create today's reading programs. And they are not unrepresentative of the kind of questions raised by school and community groups.

There are other important concerns that also impinge on decisions—both the decisions made by publishers to publish and those made by teachers to use. Many relate to the legitimate concerns of particular groups of parents and citizens—in some cases, citizens who hold values different from those of the prevailing majority but whose views must, nevertheless, be respected and considered by our schools. Among such troubling concerns, we recently have been dealing with these:

- Excessive violence in readers is a concern to many parents, but determining what is excessive is the real concern to publishers. Should Odysseus' encounter with Polyphemus be eliminated from sixth grade readers because the Cyclopes kills several of the wanderer's crew?
- Nudity is anathema in many forms but is it "nudity" in *Call It Courage* when the Polynesian boy is seen swimming clad only in his *loincloth*? Should he be fully clothed?

Inclusion of science fiction and stories of witchcraft and the occult appear to encounter increased resistance in direct proportion to the rising student interest in such reading.

Demands are mounting for greater reliance on "standard edited English" in the dialogue and narrative of the readers, just as teachers are discovering the uses of natural language—that is, informal English similar to that spoken by the child—in furthering important instructional purposes.

Theories of evolution and creation, attitudes toward American values and ideals, points of view on business and labor, respect for the law, positive relationships between parents and children, treatments of religion or perceived religious issues, views on poverty and slum conditions, depiction of living conditions in other parts of the world (particularly those cultures from which sizeable groups of American ethnics have descended), the treatment of Jewish cultural history including presentation of the Holocaust, and political attitudes of various persuasions are among the more sensitive issues today.

How do publishers balance the wide variety of demands and still create viable programs which satisfy instructional requirements and, at the same time, provide books that children want to read?

1. They depend on large groups of authors, editors, and designers whose own ethnic mix and values represent the very plurality of values the programs are attempting to achieve.
2. They develop staff training programs and create detailed guidelines to assist editors and designers in handling

those critical concerns. For example, major publishers have established rigorous guidelines to avoid overt racist and sexist bias.

3. They interact continuously with customers throughout the country to determine the prevailing attitudes of the schools. When it appears that a broad consensus has been reached, the publisher will take significant action. It is not likely that a responsible publisher would eliminate a particular selection or specific illustration merely because vocal dissenters in a single community objected to its inclusion. But if that selection creates difficulties in school situations throughout the nation, it probably should be replaced.

4. They field test many selections in appropriate communities of various kinds to obtain reactions from both pupils and teachers.

5. They employ groups of independent consultants to advise on dimensions and aspects of content and illustration that require technical expertise—how to authentically portray an Arab mosque or a Hopi dwelling.

But, in the final analysis, the publisher must make the final decision, weighing conflicting recommendations from a variety of well meaning and well informed sources. Would you, for example, depict an Iroquois child in moccasins when your Native American adviser insists such depiction is authentic but some customers see such illustrations as stereotypic? Would you include "Jack and the Beanstalk" in a reader knowing that some parents see the tale as advocating thievery? Should you show a pioneer family seeking food with a matchlock gun, knowing today's sensitivities to depiction of firearms of any kind? Such issues are not easy to resolve.

To what extent do these pressures on publishers constitute censorship and/or indoctrination, either before or after publication? Or to what extent do they merely reflect the complex and often conflicting concerns of the constituency our schools and publishers must serve?

Any responsible publisher seeks to provide classrooms with material of quality which can be used under a variety of classroom conditions. He recognizes that programs of many different kinds are needed and that all cannot be as one. The local communities must decide. He is further willing to submit his material to the closest possible scrutiny by educational and community leaders, although he asks that these processes be clearly defined and administered with careful regard to "due process" to ensure that a particularly militant minority does not impose its will on the majority to the detriment of the learning of boys and girls. Affirmative action cannot and must not be turned into affirmative discrimination.

A publisher will also make mistakes, despite the many precautions undertaken in the development of his programs and, when he recognizes his mistakes, he stands ready to correct them.

A responsible publisher's major consideration is the development of quality material to serve the instructional needs of classrooms. To the extent that he allows the great variety of pressures and concerns to distract him from seeing that the major purpose of a reading program is to help children learn to read, he will have abandoned his central mission. But to the extent he neglects the widespread concerns, he will find that his program, however superb its instructional effectiveness, will seldom be used in the classroom.

Part Three

Parent and Teacher Perspectives

While the papers in the preceding section express the *producer's* viewpoint, Part 3 contains some *consumer* oriented parent and educator viewpoints. Segraves' paper is an articulate example of a parent actively involved in legal efforts to have schools present both secular and sacred viewpoints. Her assertion that schools should present both humanistic and theistic world views deserves careful consideration. Next, Hatcher presents an educator's rationale and some guidelines for mediating polarized positions and making curriculum decisions in a pluralistic society. And finally, after explaining the need for parents and educators to trust each other, Erickson describes a number of practical, trust-building practices that thoughtful educators are using to maintain cooperation and understanding between home and school.

The Children of the Second Generation

Nell J. Segraves

SEPARATION OF CHURCH AND STATE

Over the past several generations, separation of church and state decisions have been interpreted to mean a separation of the state from God. With the help of the media, these court decisions and interpretations have been given wide dissemination leading to the common belief that tax supported institutions may not give any recognition to God and to religious beliefs.

As a result, public education has been secularized in both teacher training and choice of curriculum studies from kindergarten through the university level. Some parents now fear that their children have been, in effect, made "wards of the state" because these state systems disregard the religious and cultural beliefs of the parents in the education of their children. Parents are left with tax support of the schools but with no jurisdiction over the schools. As a result of the noninvolvement of parents in the past two generations, children now in school are products of a system in which state, home, and church have all been affected by secularization. Homes and schools have become battlegrounds for two opposing philosophies—the one founded on absolute moral standards answering to God and His word, and the other on a state mandated philosophy of relative morals based on whatever society currently is accepting.

On the one hand, a child is taught to obey God's commandments. On the other hand, he is taught that he is a law unto himself and can determine right and wrong; accept responsibility for himself alone; and not answer to his parents, church, government, or to God.

The state now sits in the position of Solomon when he viewed two mothers claiming ownership of the same child. Solomon, in wisdom, took a sword and held the child as if to cut it in half, giving one-half to each one claiming ownership. The rightful mother cried out in anguish, "No, give the child to the other woman, don't destroy it." Solomon then took the child and placed it in the arms of the true mother, knowing only a real parent would not sacrifice her child at the expense of her own love. But our state system—lacking the wisdom of Solomon, whose wisdom came from God—declares war on parents over the teaching and training of the children.

A NEW STATE RELIGION

Since it is impossible to separate subject matter from a philosophical interpretation, or world view, parents feel that the only way to correct the present problems is to ask for a balanced presentation of both basic points of view. A one-sided presentation in the classroom, based on one philosophy or world view, tends to indoctrinate the student to accept and believe the one philosophy as the only true and correct one. The practice of preferential treatment by the state is a violation of the First Amendment (establishment of religion clause) and the Fourteenth Amendment (equal protection clause) to the United States Constitution. The famous Supreme Court decision of 1963 stated that secularism of the public schools is unconstitutional. Justice Goldberg also pointed out that "the attitude of the state toward religion must be one of neutrality," and that even neutrality can lead to results that are actively hostile to the religious and, therefore, are unconstitutional.

THE AGE OF REBELLION

Angered and frustrated by their lack of control, parents go to the polls and vote down one bond issue after another, feeling this to be the only outlet for their frustrations. School boards in local areas pass responsibility to the state and national levels, not wanting to get involved in legal action. Children, seeing the discord between home and school, take it upon themselves to throw over all authority. This reaction spilled into the streets during the 1960s. The all important questions, "Why are we here?" and "Where are we going?" are left unanswered. Children become the objects of a warfare as destructive as any known. The results are open rebellion and chaos in America with fear of children rampant in most, if not all, of America's big cities.

HOW DO WE RETURN TO A WORLD OF LAW AND ORDER?

In desperation, some parents take their children out of the hostile environment of public education and place them in private schools. Across America, the growth of private education has astonished the experts who believe in a common curriculum for all children as basic to the common good of the nation. Because of the vast amounts of tax funding available to public education, private education cannot compete. There is a realization on the part of some parents that private schools are only a partial answer and that religious freedom is really the issue at stake in this country. The majority of our citizens in America are still being educated in a philosophy hostile to religious beliefs and they can, in time, curtail religious freedom through the majority vote, even in the private sector.

THE LAW IS OUR DEFENSE

Parents, with the help of their California legislators, researched and established a legal premise as a base to solve the inequities in the educational system. This legal premise showed that:

1. Public schools may not legally promote any particular religious philosophy directly or indirectly.
2. Citizens can request, through actions of local school boards of education as well as state boards, that public schools stop promoting irreligious and atheistic doctrines.

Such a neutral position can be achieved in the schools by:

1. Allowing the objective presentation of both points of view regarding humanistic and theistic world views.
2. Forbidding the indoctrination in all subject matter that may offend cultural or religious beliefs.

The legal principle is that all children have equal rights under the law regarding protection of their religious beliefs; but, in actual application, the present censorship of Biblical views is "severely, if not totally" destructive of the religious liberties of Christian children. To restrict the teaching to humanistic views as the only acceptable world view violates the Constitutional prohibition against the teaching of sectarian religious views just as clearly as if the teaching concerning world views were restricted to the world view revealed in the Scriptures.

RECENT SUPREME COURT DECISIONS

We agree, of course, that the state may not establish a "religion of secularism" in the sense of showing hostility to religion, thus preferring those who believe in no religion over those who do believe....

It is said, and I agree, that the attitude of the state toward religion must be one of neutrality. But untutored devotion to the concept of neutrality can lead to invocation or approval of results which partake not simply of that noninterference and noninvolvement with the religions which the Constitution commands, but of a brooding and pervasive devotion to the secular, or even active hostility to the religious. Such results are not only not compelled by the Constitution but, it seems to me, are prohibited by it *(4)*.

The California State Board's policy statement which governs classroom teaching interprets the Supreme Court's decision in the following manner:

So if the state is forbidden by the Constitution to promote the Christian religion, it is also forbidden to promote a godless religion of secularism or atheism. It would seem to follow, therefore, that no teacher is at liberty to teach a point of view denying God any more than a teacher is at liberty to promote a particular religious sect *(1)*.

Mr. Justice Goldberg with Mr. Justice Harlan concurring says the realization of religious liberty means that the government shall effect "no favoritism among sects or between religion and nonreligion" and that it shall "work deterrence of no religious belief." These two justices go further and recognize the danger of a noninterference and noninvolvement with religion which might promote a "passive or even active hostility to the religious." Such results, says Mr. Justice Goldberg, "are not only not compelled by the Constitution but, it seems to me, are prohibited by it." It seems quite clear that the Supreme Court recognized and warned against the danger of creating passive attitudes of hostility toward religion....

The Justices' opinions in this case recognize the importance of religion and reflect a great respect for it. They are men who would not willingly weaken religion in any way nor substitute a godless philosophy for it.

The State Board of Education believes that these matters need to be brought to the attention of parents as well as to school officials. While religious worship services are not to be held in the schools nor is any religious group to be given the right to promote his particular point of view, Christian parents, therefore, are protected by law against any attempt to destroy or weaken their children's faith in their particular church. The religious faith of the majority is protected as well as the freedom of the minority.

Our schools should have no hesitancy in teaching about religion. We urge our teachers to make clear the contributions of religion to our civilization, through history, art, and ethics. We want the children of California to be aware of the spiritual principles and the faith which undergird our way of life. We are confident that our teachers are competent to differentiate between teaching about religion and conducting a compulsory worship service. This point of view, we believe, is in accordance with the tradition handed down by our fathers and reaffirmed by the United States Supreme Court *(4)*.

PARENTS REINVOLVED IN EDUCATION

As a result of California's recognition of parental right to oversee the moral and religious education of their minor children, parents have shown a willingness to become involved within the system of public education. The state board has encouraged this by providing a time frame for parent participation in the adoption process for textbooks and curriculum development and by setting forth a legal framework for a criteria statement that publishers must meet. Educators then select from books which are in legal compliance and have parent approval. This new system has proven to be workable with all parties involved.

But this is only a beginning, at the state level, in which relatively few citizen-voter-parents have as yet participated. An even more important place for their concern and active political effort is in their local school districts, with the local school boards, administrators, and classroom teachers. This is where parent apathy must be replaced by vigorous, intelligent, and constructive activity. Only thus can public schools become centers for educating productive, self-disciplined, freedom-loving citizens rather than production lines for crowds of half-literate, pleasure-seeking rebels against all authority but their own self-will.

It will take time before the classroom will benefit from the changes in educational philosophy, but the renewed interest and cooperation between educators and parents cannot help but be beneficial to our children and to the future of America.

THE ROOTS GO DEEPER

Rousas Rushdoony showed how the humanistic faith of John Locke and his clean tablet concept, Rousseau's idea of the natural man, and the materialistic frameworks of Marx, Freud, and Darwin bred hostility to discipline and obedience, thus leading to revolution. Western civilization and liberty were established on foundations of faith and discipline grounded in Christian and particularly Reformation theology. The fundamental unit of authority was the family, and the source of this authority, God. But modern permissiveness which arises when the source of this authority is forgotten undermines parental authority, prevents the growth of self-discipline, and leads to the disintegration of society or to a reign of terror. Contrary to the commonplace view of scholars, says

Rushdoony, all authority is in essence religious authority; the nature of the authority depends on the nature of the religion. If the religion is Biblical, then the authority at every point is the immediate or mediated authority of God. If the religion is humanistic, then the authority is everywhere implicitly or explicitly the autonomous consciousness of man.

"Without a valid doctrine of authority, no order stands" *(2)*.

References

1. California State Board of Education Policy Statement, December 17, 1963. Copy available from 721 Capitol Mall, Sacramento, California.
2. Rushdoony, Rousas John. *The Institutes of Biblical Law.* New Jersey: Craig Press, 1973.
3. Segraves, Nell, and Jean Sumrall. *A Legal Premise for Moral and Spiritual Guidelines for California Public Schools.* San Diego: CSRC, 1971.
4. U.S. Supreme Court Decision of June 17, 1963, *Abington School District Vs. Schempp*, Page 9, Part II. Nos. 142 and 119, October Term, 1962.

Educational Directions in a Pluralistic Society

Thomas C. Hatcher

In a pluralistic society, such as exists in the United States, the class-room teacher, the school, and the school system in general face an extremely difficult and complex curricular task. This task, encountered by most of those involved in our educational system, is that of responding to the needs, desires, and wishes of each member of our pluralistic society, some of whom might be requesting directions which are contradictory to positions held by others. As a consequence, educational leaders—and especially classroom teachers—are often thrust into untenable positions in which "losing" occurs, no matter what decision might be made in relation to a particular controversy.

For the educator, satisfying all segments of our society appears to be an impossible task since, as a nation, we are so diverse in our thinking and beliefs. Beginning with the Supreme Court decisions regarding discrimination in the 1950s, the United States has become a nation of individuals and groups who have sought to express their beliefs and philosophical values and to ultimately seek court decisions regarding those positions. While many of these court decisions have related to individual and minority rights within our society and have not been directed initially toward school systems, it is only natural to assume, given this route of seeking court opinion on controversial issues, that such a direction would ultimately affect the school and eventually be directed to it. The school, as a vehicle to maintain our society and for which total support comes from members of the society, must adhere to court decisions which affect society in general. In addition, according to the Constitution, public education must guarantee the rights of individuals and minorities since public education is supported totally by tax dollars.

Educators, who in the past have unilaterally made most of the decisions regarding educational directions, are now being bombarded with court decisions which affect education, and by individuals and groups who seek support for the presentation and/or consideration of particular philosophical beliefs and values in the educational system. Educators, caught in the middle of this public awareness and involvement direction within society (which the writer believes is a "good" one), are now thrust into extremely complex positions, in which their decisions regarding curricular directions are being scrutinized by parents, individuals, and groups in our country. The dilemma facing the educator, therefore, is one of how to proceed, given such involvement and concerns regarding educational directions and given the fact that schools are public institutions. Should the educator maintain a neutral position regarding morals, values, and beliefs, referring pupils to parents for answers? Should the educator consider the presentation of controversial moral, value, and belief issues in schools? If so, in what direction should the presentations be thrust? Should the school respond totally to the wishes of those individuals whose tax dollars support a particular school system, or does the school have an obligation to support needs and directions of our society in general, since schools are a vehicle to maintain society, and not the domain of just those who financially support a particular school system? The remainder of this paper will attempt to clarify the position of the writer (both a parent and an educator) who is requesting that the public educator listen and respond to beliefs held by the writer—beliefs which are felt to be representative of a segment of our society.

Any considerations advocated for coping with the dilemma regarding the direction of public education are very much related to the philosophical beliefs of the individual who is suggesting directions. This writer is not suggesting that the following represent ultimate answers but, rather, represent a particular point of view and, as such, should be considered by those making decisions regarding educational curricula.

GUIDELINES FOR EDUCATIONAL DESIGN IN A PLURALISTIC SOCIETY

1. *Public education is a means, within our society, for maintaining the democratic principles, directions, and decisions of our pluralistic nation.* Since the writer feels that education is a vehicle for maintaining our societal beliefs and values, then the educational system must adhere to and support those universal principles advocated by the Constitution and upheld by the courts of our land. While as individuals and/or groups we might disagree with particular decisions made by our courts (such as

some do in the removal of prayer from schools), we, as members of a democratic society, must nevertheless support such decisions or attempt to change them. Educators must assume responsibility for identifying these universal principles and for communicating them to both teachers and individuals within a particular school district (i.e., separation of church and state, nondiscrimination, respect for individual rights).

2. *Since a primary purpose of education is that of producing a rational thinking individual who can become a productive member of society, then schools must not "shy away" from the presentation of controversial societal issues in determining curricular directions.*
The pluralistic nature of our country mandates respect and consideration for individual and group rights, values, and beliefs, as long as these do not interfere with the rights of others. We are a nation of many beliefs which cannot be categorized as "right" or "wrong." If schools are means to preserve this pluralistic characteristic, then schools must present issues which might be categorized as controversial by certain groups so that individuals may develop their own values and beliefs, as well as develop respect for the values and beliefs of others. To do anything else would be contrary to the democratic, pluralistic principles on which this country was founded. The schools, as both reflector and preserver of society, must be responsible for the presentation and discussion of societal directions and problems, no matter what particular individuals or groups may feel about the right of the school to do so.

3. *Schools must develop involvement and communication strategies which insure the input of all concerned in designing curricular thrusts.*
It is assumed that, in their training, educators should have developed a sense for societal directions and for methods and techniques of presenting curricular content. It is not appropriate, however, for the educator to act unilaterally in determining curricular subject matter, methods, and techniques. Parents and others must be actively involved in curricular design and must work closely with educators in resolving any conflicts which might occur.

4. *Individuals and/or groups who hold opinions varying from prevailing trends should not automatically expect public institutions to adopt their viewpoints.*
As a member of our democratic society, I know that my views will not always be held by the majority. Since I support democratic ideals, I must accept the right of the majority to prevail, even though my beliefs are contrary. In doing so, I, *as an individual*, must resolve how to deal with this conflict. It is not through becoming a public nuisance, however, but through a rational, problem approach that I attempt to resolve conflicts. Public institutions should not be expected to adopt my views, just because I, or the group to which I belong, think we are right. In the past, individuals or groups have subjected schools and educators to unnecessary pressures because of lack of knowledge regarding school directions

emanating from societal mandates. As a parent, I must find the necessary means to support schools in fulfilling their primary responsibility—that of education. To create unnecessary pressure, due to a lack of understanding, will only aid in promoting chaos.

Educational directions in a pluralistic society are, indeed, difficult to determine. The school, if it is to reflect and promote society, must assume an *active* role in developing rational individuals who are critical and creative thinkers; who respond to change and complexity; who question and comment; and who ultimately determine their own directions, values, and beliefs. As a parent, I expect the system my children attend to support and develop the principles of our democratic, pluralistic nation, in which most of us believe, and to support the active consideration and respect for differences within our culture. As an individual within this society, I respect the rights of others to disagree and I believe that, if there are disagreements, procedures for resolving such conflicts either exist or can be developed.

Closing the Adversary Gap

Lawrence G. Erickson

In 1962, at an American Education Week open house, I became aware of the crucial need for parents and teachers to trust one another. As a rookie fifth grade teacher, with the superintendent's ten-year-old daughter in my class, I had carefully prepared for the open house. The classroom was decorated with the best samples of my students' work, and perched on the chalk tray were the different textbooks we used. I proceeded to discuss each subject with about thirty parents. Afterwards, over the inevitable PTA coffee and doughnuts, I was jolted by one father (not the superintendent) who made this sincere comment on trust: "The reason I'm here tonight is that I'm really not interested in those textbooks you presented as much as I am curious about what kind of a person you are and how you'll interact with my child."

This early lesson, as well as a multitude of experiences as teacher, principal, and parent, has led me to regard *trust* as a most powerful determinant of home-school relationships. In fact, I am convinced that confrontations, such as the recent widespread controversies over school textbooks, are but one indicator of a genuine lack of trust in American public education. Other indicators are equally indicative of this lack of trust. For example, one Washington columnist stated that President Carter's decision to send his daughter to a public elementary school is like the Old Testament story of sacrificing a first-born on the altar. What has happened? Why has trust in public schooling reached an all-time low? Why do many parents hesitate and others give up communicating with the schools their children attend? Why do many principals and teachers feel threatened when parents call or visit the school? What is this gap that exists today between home and school? The purpose of this article is to examine this estrangement and offer some alternatives for reducing what I choose to call the *adversary gap*.

As I see it, a basic issue between home and school is the adversary position both parties tend to take toward almost all interactions. By adversary, I mean that the basic assumption which prompts parent involvement is that something must be wrong for any interaction to take place. In either case, the first response from either the school or the parent has been "What is wrong?" As a principal, I vividly remember coaxing a mother to school in order to share her son's improved schoolwork and behavior. Her response was, "No sir, I'm not coming. Every time I've come in the past all I ever heard was bad news."

I have pondered this adversary gap from both sides. I feel this estrangement personally, I hear about it from others, and I see evidence in the media that it is widespread. This issue has seized my interest to the extent that I now interpret home-school conflict, such as controversy over textbooks, as evidence of deep feelings of separation. Like two armies peering over a truce line, parents and schools only interact when a violation is reported. And since there is a better-than-even chance that a report may be rumor or a genuine mistake, the truce zone widens and the two camps move farther apart, trusting each other even less than before.

What is trust between home and school, and how can it be restored in face of the adversary gap? Trust is a subtle phenomenon that is difficult to explain because of the complicated interaction which nurtures its existence. It is not my intent here to try to unravel all of its intricacies. So, at the risk of oversimplifying the concept, consider that trust is enhanced when teachers and principals can predict parent reactions to school practices, and parents can accurately predict school policies, procedures, and staff behaviors. The key idea in this definition of trust is *prediction*. For, in order to predict each other's responses, home and school need to communicate often and openly, about both positive and negative issues. Both parties have to experience success in predicting each other's responses in both good and bad situations. Frequent, accurate, and successful prediction experiences by both parties are absolutely necessary in order to establish and maintain a trusting relationship.

How does this explanation of trust apply to home and school interaction? There is no pat answer, but two obvious (though sometimes forgotten) assumptions seem particularly pertinent. First of all, because there is more good news than bad news to share between home and school, there must be a concentrated effort to shift from adversary interaction policies and procedures to planned activities which put parents and teachers together under positive conditions. For example, I think school athletic events are planned activities which parents demand because of the positive connotations inherent in sports activities. Additional activities are needed which highlight other aspects of school life such as the academic achievements of all students or the excellent behavior of the majority of students. How about involving the mayor, PTA, board of education, superintendent, and textbook selection committee in a ceremony to celebrate the adoption of a new basal reader? We celebrate a ground breaking for a new school—aren't books as important as bricks?

A second assumption is that educators at the local school level bear the brunt of the responsibility for initiating new procedures, changing old policies, and actively seeking to teach the community how to act less as adversaries and more as partners. To assume that parents don't want to interact as partners will become a self-fulfilling prophecy. Over the years, my interest in trust has prompted me to keep track of school activities which seem to promote nonadversary interaction. Here is a sample of some trust building ideas that principals and teachers currently use.

1. Teachers report good news to the principal and, each week, the principal makes at least two "good news" phone calls to parents.
2. Teachers send children to the office for doing well or showing improvement. Children have frequent experiences with the principal based on positive, not only adversary, circumstances.
3. Children are involved, when appropriate, in parent-teacher conferences. Apparently, when children see that home and school agree, commitment and involvement are greatly enhanced.
4. School conferences for all parents are arranged at least twice a year. Having conferences for only those who "need" them is viewed strictly as an adversary policy which tends to promote estrangement.
5. A newsletter, which tells of school events and activities, is sent home every Friday to help parents predict what will be happening. In addition, reporting everyday activities, anecdotes, lost and found items, examples of children's writing, and other mundane but realistic news paints an accurate picture of what schools are all about.

6. Parents are involved as volunteers in the classrooms and as helpers and supervisors in the lunchroom and playground. Parent "experts" come to school to talk, demonstrate, teach their skills, and contribute their ideas.

7. Parents run errands, type, collate, staple, save pictures, and carry out other support services at home.

8. Teacher and/or principal-parent coffees are held in parents' homes. Meeting parents in their homes builds trust more quickly than requiring parents to visit the school.

9. Clearly written explanations about *How We Teach Beginning Reading and Here is What You Can Do to Help, Our Homework Policy*, or other school activities are sent home to let parents predict what the school expects. The most useful messages (policies) are usually written by a committee of parents and teachers.

10. Classes are arranged to show parents what things they can do at home to help their children learn. Schools which have seriously attempted this, report remarkable changes in home-school relationships and improved pupil achievement.

11. Individual teachers feel free and are encouraged to have their own parent meetings frequently throughout the year. All-school PTA meetings are usually not personal enough to allow parents and teachers to interact in meaningful ways.

12. An end-of-year school closing ceremony is held during which the American flag is lowered. The ceremony is short and all of the parents who have volunteered during the year come and receive a certificate and an award for their contributions.

Obviously, this is only a small sample of the kinds of school initiated activities which are most helpful in reducing the adversary gap. None of them succeeds alone nor do all work the first few times they are tried. And, certainly, nothing replaces good teaching or good administration. But instructional excellence is more easily demonstrated through planned activities which bring home and school together in a concentrated effort to focus on the good things that are taking place. What about negative things, such as distasteful books or poor teaching? Of course such problems exist and they cannot be ignored; but, in too many instances, negative events have been the primary basis for interaction and discussion.

As a result, an adversary gap exists which has spawned mistrust. School personnel at the local level can begin reducing the adversary gap by actively seeking to engage in trust building activities. To ignore this need is to miss an important chance for preventing further deterioration of public education.

Part Four

Textbook Adoption:
Criteria and Procedures

Given the pluralistic and often conflicting viewpoints of parents and educators, how can schools select materials which not only protect but even nurture individuality? Erickson and Fomalont suggest that materials should be selected on the basis of broad school and community goals rather than only on the basis of pedagogical considerations. Lohr describes an example of one school district's comprehensive selection procedures. Her description of an actual procedure for handling controversial materials and her case studies of selection practices deserve careful reading by educators who desire to improve their selection policies and procedures.

Criteria for the Evaluation of Reading Materials

Lawrence G. Erickson and Michele M. Fomalont

Before considering some criteria for the evaluation of reading materials, it is worthwhile to reflect that the process of selecting such materials is greatly enhanced when a school has a well-formulated reading philosophy with accompanying objectives. Such a philosophy can be developed only after student, teacher, administrator, and community needs and expectancies have been carefully considered and assessment has been made of the school's present reading program, including its strengths and weaknesses. All individuals who are concerned with meeting these needs and expectancies must be given the opportunity to participate in the discussions. Teachers, administrative personnel, and community representatives (including parents and even the school children) should contribute their opinions and evaluations. The specific needs of pupils at all levels, the competencies of all staff members, and the expectations of the community as to what the reading program will do all need to be considered.

Without a reading philosophy developed in this way, a materials selection committee will find itself simply comparing one text or one basal series with another on the basis of internal criteria; that is, factors which for the most part are already present in the materials themselves. There are numerous checklists in existence which bear witness to the fact that this is commonly the case. For example, a typical question included in such a checklist is, "Does the proposed series stress reading for meaning?" Members of a selection committee are expected to rate the proposed series or text according to how well they believe this objective is accomplished. The only problem is, for just about any basal found on the market today, the answer to this question would be a high-rated "yes." This is a compliment to the publisher but is of little help to the committee in making a choice.

On the other hand, if a school tests its students and finds they need help with developing study skills, yet lack motivation to read nonfiction stories, then a series could be judged on how well it provides for study skills without relying solely on content stories, or it could be judged for the relevance of its motivational devices. This is just one example of how a committee might examine proposed materials on the basis of both internal and external criteria—in this case, the needs of its own students.

Let's assume that the school or school system has defined its overall reading goals which inherently include its own particular student, teacher, administrator, and community concerns. The next step is to find materials which will facilitate the implementation of these goals. One way to overcome the problem of simply rating textbooks according to internal criteria is to formulate questions which test whether the proposed materials will satisfy the defined reading goals. Following are some areas common to materials checklists that might be considered, keeping the school's objectives in mind. Questions can be grouped according to community, school, and classroom concerns.

COMMUNITY

- Is presentation of ethnic groups, sex roles, controversial issues, and current issues consistent with community expectations?
- Is there evidence to show that the series has been field tested and the results used in the development of the publication? Do the field tests include communities whose needs are similar to those of the community where the materials are being considered?

SCHOOL

- Is the philosophy of the series concerning the approach to the teaching of reading consistent with the school's definition of reading?
- Is administration of the proposed series consistent with the school's management plans?

CLASSROOM

- How does the series provide for the evaluation of the skills presented, both readiness and posttesting?
- How can a teacher use the series to teach a specific skill or cater to a particular interest?

- Is the treatment of word attack, comprehension, study skills, interpretation, and creative activities consistent with the school's objectives at different levels?
- What motivational devices are used to encourage assigned and independent reading?
- How can the teacher individualize instruction using the series? Is there provision for corrective, adapted, and accelerated teaching?
- How does the series provide for a wide range of interests about many different topics? Does it include a balance of reading material and literary forms (realistic, fanciful, humorous, serious, factual, fictional, poetic, biographical, contemporary, traditional)?

Answers to questions such as these will not only indicate how well textbooks and materials meet different internal criteria, they will also help the staff to decide whether the materials are consistent with the external criteria such as the school philosophy and school goals. Of course, the process is not always as cut-and-dried as it has been presented here. Many times school philosophy is clarified by the selection of materials, or development of a school's reading philosophy and study of materials are carried on simultaneously. The main consideration always should be that the school's goals define the materials, rather than that the materials define the school program.

ERICKSON and FOMALONT

Materials Selection Processes: Why and How?

Elaine Lohr

When American students enter school, they enter a reading culture. From the beginning they are expected to learn to read; learn to gain information from what they read; and learn to make inferences, state conclusions, and evaluate what they read. It is also likely that the students enter schools that have a written statement of education which proposes to train all students to become successful members of a democratic society. To this end, it is generally held that the students need to become independent thinkers and be able to analyze ideas, to weigh alternative points of view, and to make sound decisions.

Textbooks abound; students are required to read. "The...cat ...is...fat." "Turn to page 65 and answer the questions at the bottom of the page." "Read pages 608 to 732 for the test tomorrow." "Read at least three references and write a twelve page report." "Sara, it's your turn. What, you don't know where we are?" "It's time for quiet reading." "How did you feel when you read that?" "I don't know, Bill, how could your find out?" "George Washington wore wooden false teeth." "Read the statement that supports what you just said." "Read!"

For many teachers, the textbook becomes the mainstay of their curriculum. For many students, the textbook becomes the basis of "their work." Textbooks can become ends in themselves, purchased from a persuasive sales person, seized at a book fair because of the colorful pictures or the self-correcting workbook pages, embraced because "we have always used that book," or assigned so "the kids have something to do." But the textbook must not be an end in itself, a necessary evil, a crutch. It must be selected to help support well defined purposes of the curriculum.

The Madison, Wisconsin, Public Schools have developed a materials selection policy which supports the concept of the right to free choice among alternatives of a free society and the rational development of the instructional program. The district policy provides guidelines for all staff to follow. Those closest to the instructional program should be responsible for identifying curriculum goals, strategies, and materials. However, it is equally important that the general criteria for the school district be followed in order to insure the fulfillment of the basic philosophy of the materials selection policy. Each materials selection committee then is responsible for developing a specific process which best fits its area of the instructional program, while working within the framework of the school district's general policy.

The selection committee is asked to state instructional goals and to consider such aspects of texts as format, durability, readability, authoritativeness, and quality of writing. It is understood, however, that the major areas of controversy are race, sex, politics, religion, literature, and economics. Therefore, the following criteria are provided as guidelines (3):

1. The materials on controversial issues should be representative of a particular point of view and a sincere effort to select equally representative materials covering contrasting points of view.
2. The material does not unfairly, inaccurately, or viciously disparage a particular race or religion. A writer's expression of a certain viewpoint is not to be considered a disparagement when it represents the historical or contemporary views held by some persons or groups.
3. The materials on religion are chosen to explain rather than convince and are selected to represent the field as widely as necessary for the school purposes.
4. The selection of materials on political theories and ideologies or public issues is directed toward maintaining a balanced collection representing various views.
5. In a literary work of established quality, the use of profanity or the treatment of sex is not an adequate reason for eliminating the material.
6. Materials on physiology, physical maturation, or personal hygiene should be accurate and in good taste.
7. Materials should be selected for their strengths rather than rejected for their weaknesses.

The material selection policy provides a procedure for community members to respond to the materials selected. A systematic method for registering and addressing concerns is as follows *(3)*:

1. The complainant shall submit the Complainant Request for Reconsideration of Instructional Materials form to the principal of the school involved for consideration by the principal, librarian, and/or school staff.
2. The challenged materials will be reevaluated by the media professional staff, the principal, and the advisory staff, including the person making the original selection, if possible.
3. If it is the desire of the complainant, the request shall be submitted to the area director for consideration.
4. Following consideration by the area director, if it is the desire of the complainant, it shall be submitted to the superintendent for consideration.

The importance of this procedure is, first, that it places responsibility on those who are selecting the materials. It directs that they must consider the *why* of what they want to select: that is, they decide what they want to teach, why they want to teach it, and *then* select materials which provide for the instructional goals as well as the rights of the individual in a pluralistic society. Second, the selection policy requires that persons who question material must assume responsibility for reviewing and explaining their objections. Under the selection policy, text materials may not be added or subtracted on a whim or a snap judgment. This policy, then, is the basis for a rational process of both selecting and challenging instructional materials.

COMMITTEE CASE STUDIES

To provide the reader with a better understanding of the workings of materials selection committees in Madison, three case studies will be described: Program Materials Selection (PMS), the Analysis of Reading Materials Selection (ARMS) procedure, and the Middle School/High School Paperback Committee. The PMS process is one that is used by the individual teacher or teacher committees to apply for and secure instructional materials which will form a foundation or core curriculum. The first step of the procedure requires the applicants to document the program they are either currently teaching or are intending to introduce into the curriculum. Before materials are examined, the program documentation must communicate four points: 1) the goals of the program, 2) how these goals meet the needs of the students, 3) a description of any materials currently available, and 4) the adequacy of these materials for the instructional program. This step in the process underscores the belief that the first step in text selection is to establish *why* it is important to have new materials for a program. The second step in the process is the review of materials. At this time, teachers evaluate the materials to see if they are strong enough to meet the instructional goals and also meet human relations and readability criteria.

The Human Relations Department of the Madison Public Schools has developed an instrument for the evaluation of instructional materials for social bias, analyzing sexual and racial roles depicted in print and illustrations *(2)*. In addition, the department provides workshops designed to help teachers be more aware of the effect of social bias in materials and to suggest methods for supplementation of unbalanced material. Teachers may purchase additional supplementary materials or provide instruction regarding prejudicial materials that may be included in the text to bring about balance of presentation.

An additional evaluation is required of all materials regarding the readability of those texts. It is recognized that materials may meet and provide for a balanced human relations presentation, yet be too difficult for students to read. The last step in gaining necessary material is to submit all program and evaluation documentation to the Board of Education, which makes the final authorization for the purchase of textbooks.

A second selection process, the Analysis of Reading Materials Scale (ARMS), has been developed specifically for analyzing reading materials in the elementary schools of the East Attendance Area *(1)*. This process, developed by a group of teachers and principals during the past two years, provides a set of criteria which allows the elementary schools in the area the freedom to select materials needed for their particular students and yet support the common reading goals developed for all the students in the East Attendance Area. Three categories are included in the scale: 1) items which provide for the analysis of the skills that are purportedly taught through the text material; 2) management analysis which applies to the way the teacher manual, workbooks, and tests are developed and manipulated within a classroom; and 3) balance of content scale which allows for analysis of an integrated language arts focus and the inclusion of emphasis on "self and others." The ARMS evaluation scale provides for a qualitative, indepth analysis of material, helping to avoid the "pretty picture" or "favorite skill" syndrome of selecting texts. The scale focuses on the relationship of material to the goals of the reading curriculum.

Many teachers were anxious to be on the reading materials committee because they thought they would examine many new books, but they found they needed to develop criteria for "looking." One of the teachers, a twenty-five-year veteran, spoke about the rating scale to a group of her colleagues. She said that she had been won over; she had not known what was needed to make responsible textbook selection. A believer in a particular basal text, she had used it for several years and was convinced that it was *the* best. When she applied the rating scale to the text, she found her favorite series lacking in meeting some of the goals to which she ascribed. It was important for her to make this statement to other teachers because it indicated to them the awareness level that one could have if one carefully analyzed teaching materials that are so important to the instructional program.

The third case study of text selection is the process used by the Middle and High School Paperback Committee. Begun in 1964, the paperback program is an integral part of the regular language arts and literature study. The purpose of the paperback program is to provide current literature or titles that would not be included in texts because of the somewhat benign character of many anthologies. A committee of teachers reviews and annotates the paperback books which may be selected by teachers for their students; it does not have the role of censoring. Committee members bring recommendations for reviews from fellow faculty members and from their own reading. Strengths and weaknesses of suggested titles are discussed before decisions are made on a book's placement in the catalog. Annotations are meant only to guide the teacher's paperback selection. For example, some books which are included might be inappropriate in certain school communities or for less mature students. Teachers are urged not only to read the annotations, but also to read the books before ordering. The paperback policy does not, however, prohibit teachers from ordering paperback books which are not in the catalog.

The purpose of the Middle/High School Paperback Catalog is to provide teachers with a wide range of reading material from which to select for students. The committee reviews the catalog frequently to be certain that selections are made which appeal to various ages and interests, which take into account the positive roles of males and females in our society, and which are representative of racial groups. The committee members, as might be expected, are avid readers who enjoy sharing with other teachers their excitement about what they read.

Perhaps the easiest part of a materials selection procedure is defining it; applying it is more difficult. All members of the school system need to be aware of the importance of the procedure and use it in a dynamic way. The school system must avoid becoming complacent, looking for loopholes, not allowing time, bending too quickly to pressure to remove a book, and selecting noncontroversial materials as avoidance.

To maintain an effective process a system should systematically review its selection procedure, answering the following questions:

1. Do we have a well-defined selection policy?
2. Do members of the staff and community use the policy?
3. Does the process require the establishment of the *why* of the curriculum before the *what*?
4. Are the selected materials sensitive to the pluralistic society?
5. Are choices rationally selected and then adequately defended (or do we bend easily to avoid controversy)?

References

1. "Analysis of Reading Materials Scale," Madison, Wisconsin, Public Schools, 1976.
2. "Breaking through Barriers in Words and Pictures," Human Relations Department, Madison, Wisconsin, Public Schools, 1974.
3. "Materials Selection Policy," Madison, Wisconsin, Public Schools, 1976 (revised).

Afterword

Although the title *Indoctrinate or Educate?* implies a choice, there is little doubt that future textbook selection and usage practices in schools will continue, as they always have, to involve both indoctrination and education. Furthermore, continued cultural diversity and rapid social changes will cause schools to remain active arenas for community control. School leaders, therefore, cannot afford to underestimate cultural divergence or rates and types of changing values. More than ever, school leaders need to initiate carefully conceived textbook guidelines. More than ever, school officials need to communicate with various interested groups in order to conceive ways in which to balance indoctrination with education. And finally, more than ever before, both educators and the public need to be better prepared to rationally determine and defend textbook policies that reflect the plurality which exists in every community and classroom in the United States.